Letitia's Thoughts in Verse

———◦~❦~◦———

LETITIA LORDE

ISBN 978-1-0980-2544-1 (paperback)
ISBN 978-1-0980-2545-8 (digital)

Christian Faith Publishing, Inc.
832 Park Avenue
Meadville, PA 16335
www.christianfaithpublishing.com

Printed in the United States of America

Contents

Acknowledgments

I want to acknowledge my husband, Clifford, who has been a solid rock upon which I could lean through the years, and whose words of wisdom have remained with me, and have stayed fixed during my past illness.

I also want to acknowledge my parents, Moses and Laura Lorde. They ensured that my brother and I received the upbringing that has allowed me to reach this stage in my life, where I can share my thoughts with the readers.

A Person

Who am I?
I'm a child of the Creator.
And who is the Creator?
He is God, the omnipotent.

What am I?
I'm a human being on earth
Sent here by the Creator
With other human beings to dwell
And to enjoy his handiworks.

From where have I come?
From the invisible to the visible
Shaped in God's image and likeness.
He created all things great, and small
And all that inhabit the earth.

How was I made?
By the works of the Almighty
Through the genes of man and woman
Known as a father and a mother
I arrived on this planet, earth.

Why are we here?
To enjoy what the Creator has made.
To marvel at His handiwork.
To praise and glorify His name.

Thoughts

These thoughts that come from me
Flowed freely because of the reality
That the Father has allowed me to be
Alive, and has set my thoughts free.

Peace to me comes because of this.
I cannot say that I will miss
Expressing my emotions to you.
For God will surely see me through.

The thoughts that I encounter each day
Are parts of my life that I can truly say.
I give the Almighty thanks, and I pray
My positive thoughts will not go away.

A Light

She has a strong desire to write.
Through her thoughts, to shine a light
For whom the future appears dim
And open their minds, let light come in.

She does her best and perseveres
To show that other people care.
Describes their needs, and how they feel
Strives, their emotional wounds to heal.

She may appear to be too kind.
But that is the desire of her mind:
To be helpful by what she writes
And to others, shine a bright light.

A light shining as bright as it can be.
To be a guide and let people see
The beacon beckoning them to follow
The straight path to a bright tomorrow.

My Reason

I want you to see
The reason I write this poetry.
It expresses through me
How sad or happy one can be.

The words that I write
May be wrong or may be right.
I may not be bright
But my words may shine a light.

My expressions may be sad.
Or the words may make you feel glad
That, by chance, you might have had
The opportunity to avoid what is bad.

Some poetic words may soothe your mind
Deter you from being unkind
And in some way, help you find
How you can deal with mankind.

I find peace in what I write.
Else, I may not see the light
That is shining, though it is out of sight
And I may lose the fight.

The fight to do what is right.
Help you and others see the light.
And, through my poetry, make you glad
To do what is good and not what is bad.

Poetry

The world is filled with poetry
That can come from you or me.
Our words that are written down in ink
Can influence how other people think.

We only need to look around
And in everything can be found
Something special to write about
Or from our lips, our feelings shout.

We tell the world how we feel.
Express our thoughts with great zeal.
And on paper, write the words
That others can copy or forward.

It is a door to discovery of things.
The words that are read can bring
Mystery to reality, and we discover
That with poetry, we enchant each other.

What Story

When I write this story
I hope to send your imagination
Rolling over the hills
And down the valleys.
And hope you will enjoy my story.

I put this story into poetry
Hoping that you will see
The reality of what one can express.
I will state as much as I can
While you imagine the injustice to man.

Starting with "Once upon a Time"
Will send thoughts flowing through your mind
As I describe my pain and sorrow
And let you wait for the completion—
Tomorrow!

Our Thoughts

Thinking can cause joy or sadness
It can also lead to madness.
It can lead to positive ideas.
Ideas can lead to inventions.

Positive thoughts can send your mind reeling
Or lead to that negative feeling
Our thoughts can lead to, "Aha! I've got it!"
Or cause the negative, "What? Not that!"

Thinking can lead to positive actions
A willingness to care for the sick
Feed the hungry, donate to the needy
And comfort the sad and lonely.

Question

Can one appear to be perfect but
Be imperfect?
Can a person be bad but
Be good?
Can someone be unkind, yet
Be kind?

The Maker of the universe is perfect.
Yet at times we question what we see.
The Creator of all living things is perfect.
Yet many things appear to go wrong.
The Almighty lasts forever!
The works of the Creator make us marvel.

Just think of planet earth!
There is no stability!
There are earthquakes, volcanoes
Windstorms, poisonous gases,
Shaping and reshaping
What was already formed!
Who is causing the changes?
The One and only One!
The forever! And forever!
The unseen but felt!
The Creator is perfect.
We will be changed from body to spirit!

Never Too Late

It is never too late
To pull yourself together
Survive the stormy weather
Be tolerant of each other.
It is not too late
To show love for another
Forgive, talk, and discover
The values of our neighbors.

It is never too late
To love all creatures
Show respect for each other
And thank our Heavenly Father.

Sadness

The melancholy that we feel is sadness.
If it is not eased, it can lead to madness.
The loss of reality, the lack of trust
Can take control and destroy us.

Sadness, oh what a sad word!
It can make one feel out of this world.
The joy for living becomes so lacking
It can send excitement packing.

Energy is lost when one is sad.
Life has no meaning, and that is bad.
So what can one do when sadness comes?
Take flight, escape the sadness, and run!

Run in the rain! Run in the sun!
Seek friends who will help you have fun.
Breathe deeply, take in fresh air
Move your limbs, pretend you don't care.

Think of people who are sad, but not mad
For who have overcome, be glad!
What are they doing, what did they do?
The person who knows is God, not you!

A Flower and a Smile

A flower can make you smile.
It can brighten your day.
It brings joy to your soul.
It is a messenger from God.
Plant a flower in your heart!
And send it to others.
The sick
The lonely
And to those who are grieving.
You may not see their smile
But their hearts may be filled with joy.
Hurry! They are waiting!

Peace

Is your mind disturbed and
You can't do your best?
Is your heart racing, even
When you are at rest?
Are you tossing and turning
When you lay in your in bed?
If so, what is going on in your head?
Peace comes when the mind is content.
Free from worry, the mind is at rest.
Free from hunger, the body is fed
Then man can say: "I'm relaxed in bed!"

Imagination

There is an invisible engine
That can bring ideas to fruition.
If you have a notion
You can put your test into motion.

Think of how, when, where, and why.
Then you can gather information, and try
To apply the thoughts your mind occupies
And invent an object that people will buy.

Use the spider as an example.
Observe its network as your sample.
Take your idea, and find a way
To invent something for which people will pay.

With success, your joy will soar high.
You will want to reach for the sky.
Your idea can lead to an invention
That can become real, due to your imagination.

Decision

Life is how you make it
You can take it, or leave it
Or you can make it, or, break it
However you consider it.

Think about it all day
Whatever you may do, or, say.
There is no other way.
So make a decision with little delay
Else, for your mistake you pay.

It is time to see the light
Or to choose between day or night
It is no good putting up a fight
Try to make your future bright.
So persevere because you have the right.

Worry

The worrier has no friend.
The plight of the worrier has no end.
What will happen today?
No one can say.
What will happen tomorrow?
Perhaps it will not bring sorrow.
Whatever is to be will be will be!

Tears

Why do we shed tears?
Is it because we have fears?
Or is it the lack of receiving loving care?
The care that we long to feel
The care that comes from hearts of steel.

An Experience

An experience can build you up
Or it can pull you down.
It can make you feel
You are wearing a crown.

The feeling you get when you discover
The joy life gives, through the beauty of nature
From sadness you can surely recover
And give praises to your Heavenly Father.

Even if you have no mother
Or you long to know your father
Your thoughts and observations of nature
Will be your comfort, don't be bothered!

Why Anger

The feeling of anger
Can make one want to spite
That person of goodwill
And that is not right.

The show of anger
Is an attitude
That can eventually
Lead to ingratitude

The lack of understanding
For the cause of the confusion
Can make the angry person
Aggravate the situation.

So let the anger end!
Think clearly, pause, and try to mend
The cause of the friction
And make that person a true friend.

Temptation

Temptation comes in different ways.
If we yield to it, then, we must pay.
Our desire to do right or wrong
Can be very weak or very strong.

We may be tempted to do bad.
And that can make us very sad.
For we can put ourselves in danger
Or in prison may have to linger.

We may be tempted to do good.
Not that we must feel we should!
For the receiver of that good action
May show ingratitude, a bad reaction.

Or, the good may be so great
That the feeling turns to love, not hate.
That goodness rendered to mankind
Can improve the status of the mind.

Think clearly when temptation comes.
Send it away, tell it, "Go home!"
Let it find somewhere to roam.
For with good thoughts is where we belong.

Patience

Life may be tough.
You may find it rough
But don't let yourself say
That you've had enough.

Things may be hard
And you may feel bad.
But do not give up.
God will fill your cup.

A Prayer Group

It is a prayer group
And it consists of ladies.
They are producing fruits
As they petition the Almighty.

This group can pray.
So lend them an ear
As to God they plead for his care.
They show no fear.

With faith and not despair
Our God will hear their prayers
That float in the air
And all who listen can hear.

Faith lets this group believe
That God will not ignore their pleas
On behalf of their friends their family
And nations far across the sea.

Change

A new day has arrived!
Sunset is now sunrise.
The sun is climbing over the horizon.
It is surrounded with yellow stripes.
The beauty of those bright colors
With the blue sky in the background
Gives the reassurance of protection
From the strong rays soon to be felt.
As the day lengthens, a change occurs!
The sun is hidden as dark clouds gather.
It rains heavily as the clouds drift away
Leaving room for the sun to reappear
And there, with a broad smile
Is a rainbow!
It is wearing that beautiful coat
That we love to see.
It cheers our hearts as we gaze
And contemplate on these beautiful
Works of our Maker.

LETITIA LORDE

A Surprise

Today, as I passed by
It caught my eyes!
I stood transfixed
Looking at it.
It was a beautiful flower!
Not delicately reared, but
A "wild" flower!

Yesterday, it was absent.
Today, it is present.
From the invisible to the visible!
I did not see it
But it saw me as I passed by.
Now, it has shown its beauty
For the world and me to see.

This small beautiful flower
Was adorned with colors
That had stripes and pink dots
On their yellow skirts.

They stretched their arms out
Welcoming me
As I stooped, their beauty to see
The flower whispered in the wind:
"See how beautiful I can be?"

I looked at its beauty
And felt the joy that
Caused my heart to swell
With a gratitude
That immediately changed
My attitude
To what is known as a "wild" flower.

It was made by our Creator
And he saw that it was good.
For God is good!
Give Him thanks!
I hope that tomorrow
A flower will greet me
With its beautiful petals.

Wonders

The moon looked on and was patient
As white, puffy clouds covered its crescent
While they slowly beneath it sailed
Making their color to viewers appear pale.

The stars that twinkled in the night
Accompanied the moon as it shone its light.
Their gift to earth was a wonderful sight
As they worked together with delight.

The wonders that are in the skies
Cannot be hidden from our eyes.
These heavenly sights make us understand
That marvel we must at what God has done.

Happiness

We know that the best things in life are free.
That God made them for you and me.
He knew that we would need company
While on this earth, where we roam free.

He has given us eyes to see the things
That joy, to us, they often bring.
We take them for granted and overlook
The greatness of God, the time He took.

He watches as we waste and disregard
His handiworks, and that is bad.
Instead, we concentrate on material things
That, at times, sadness to our hearts brings.

One of His best gifts we cannot see.
He has placed inside of you and me.
It is called "love," and it gives happiness
So that our hearts can be filled with bliss.

Write

I love to write!
Inspirational thoughts!
Thoughts that are deep.
I love to describe!
Blue skies, white clouds
Deep-blue oceans and pink sand.
Green grass beneath beautiful flowers
As they sway in the breeze.
Yes, I like the warm sun
That gives that lovely tan
That is given to us, humans.
I like the sound of the waves
As they dash against the cliffs
With large white foams.
It makes me want to go home!
Yes! I write of my homeland
It is part of Mother Earth

Observing and Thinking

Sometimes we think that all is well
But
At times we also question
The unexpected
That change our thoughts.
Why?
We wake up and are joyful to see the sun is
Shining!
It is a warm day.
The birds are singing!
There are butterflies on flowers, and
The bees are
Humming as they move from
Flower to flower, competing with the butterflies.
The sky is blue.
The clouds are white.
The grass is green.
We feel that we are blessed.
There is food in the cupboard.
Our bills have been paid.
The children have grown up, and
Our responsibilities have been eased.
Then, unexpectedly
The clouds have become gray!
The skies have darkened.
The weather has gone from warm to cold.
The flowers have withered!
The butterflies and bees have gone away.

Winter is here!
The grass has lost its green color.
It will soon be gone entirely
And will be covered with snow.
But
We are still blessed, and
Life can still be glorious!
We are alive to tell everyone about
Our observations and thoughts on the
Wonderful works of nature.
Everything is for a season, but
Life goes on!

The Yellow Moon

Before it is over
This month of October
I will overcome this gloom
Of death and doom
And joy in my heart will loom
As I look at the yellow moon.

It will not be an ordinary moon
But will be a harvest moon!
The bright yellow that I will see
Fills my heart with glee.
It will be a gift from God to us.
Give praise to God, we must
For allowing us alive, to be
And the harvest moon to see.

Companions

When I was just a little girl
I had no toys with which to play.
Had no friend with whom to talk
To make me laugh, or with me walk
Birds, bees, and butterflies made my day.

At times, I looked up at the sky
And watched the birds as they flew by.
I called to them, greeting them by name
Saying, "Birdie, bring back a doll for me!"
But knew I could not on them rely.

My garden had beautiful flowers
I imagined they were my friends.
I saw them dance from side to side.
From the wind they could not hide.
That sight I did not want to end.
I listened to the whistling wind
And the humming of the bees.
They sang with utter contentment
As they gathered nectar from flowers
And paid no attention to me.

They were followed by some butterflies
That fluttered past me without a sound
Then they gently landed on petals
Taking from nature what they found.
And I welcomed them as my companions.

I had found my childhood friends
I looked forward to their visits.
I welcomed them, one and all
Watched silently and could not call
Others to join and feel the magic.

Company

I sit on my porch
And many objects in the distance, I see.
Who are my companions?
Only my garden, the bees, and
The birds are with me.
They take away that feeling of melancholy
That can overtake one occasionally.
However, I try
To put on a smile
When the butterfly passes by
And it flutters close to my eyes.
I say to myself:
"I see you want to be in my company!
You're welcome to spend some time with me!
But you're busy like the bee
However, it's not your job to make honey."
So, I welcome those that pass me by
And that includes the annoying fly.

Alone with Nature

Why do you feel alone, my friend?
Have you no one on whom to depend?
There are many things you can do
To find the companions all around you.

Use your eyes, take in everything.
Listen to the birds as they sing.
The rustling sound of leaves on trees
As they are made restless by the breeze.

Observe the clouds as they float by.
Some appear low or very high.
Greetings to them from afar you can send as
they race ahead of the impatient wind.

Their different shapes can remind you
Of familiar objects, and things you do.
They may be gathering, this earth, to bless
With rain drops that make us want to rest.

At night, observe the cloudless sky
Where twinkling stars attract your eyes
Appearing to greet you with a smile, while
inviting you to linger with them awhile.

So do not feel alone, my friend!
Enjoy this world that will never end.
Tell your family and friends about nature
As you give joyful thanks to your Maker.

The Lonely Isle

One cannot touch loneliness.
It can be felt at times.
One cannot see loneliness
Yet, it stands out at times.

Loneliness is like an island
Surrounded by water
And, sometimes, far from another.
For people, it does not matter.

The lonely island may be big or small
It may have trees fifty feet tall.
It needs visitors to see their height
And utter: "What a wonderful sight!"

No one speaks to the lonely isle
And says, "You have tall trees!
And they have beautiful leaves!"
Rather, they plans to cut down the trees.

They take away its companions
And bring loneliness to the island.
As it stands uncovered with no other
That can call it sister or brother.

My Garden

Please excuse me, I beg your pardon
If I appear over involved in my garden.
It gives me a sense of great joy
To be among the plants that I enjoy

My garden is like a great friend.
When I'm in it, my worries end
Until I've exhausted my energy
And return to my household activity.

My plants, while in their beds, call to me.
They like me to visit them daily
To see the new blooms they have put out
And hear the words of praise from my mouth.

When I walk among the plants and flowers
I feel as if I've been visiting for hours
Discovering the secrets of Mother Nature
That attract bees, butterflies, and other creatures.

Some seek food by eating the leaves
And this causes me to become displeased.
But after considering the love of our Father
I accept their presence, it's food they're after.

Walk with Me

Come and visit me.
Let us stroll in my garden.
You will see the tropical plants.
Some have colorful flowers.
Many are the greenest ever seen.
The colors in my garden
Bring joy to my spirit.
They play with my eyes
As I marvel at their beauty.
Who made these plants and flowers?
Your Creator and nature
Made them and many more
For you and me to observe
The patterns and various colors
And feel the joys of nature.
Do you have a garden?
If you do, then take a walk in it.
Let your eyes take in the beauty.
Watch as the dew evaporates.
See how the raindrops fall on the leaves.
You will marvel at the wonders of nature
And your eyes will twinkle as you
Smile with delight.
Or they allow a tear to flow
As you realize the work of nature
That is before you.

Free for all!
So if you want to see the beauty
In spring, summer, or fall
Just give me a call!
And come walk in my garden with me.

The Rain

I loved the sound of the falling rain
As it knocked against the windowpane.
It's pattering sound, like children's feet
Kissed the earth as it greeted the street.

The showers on the roof of wood
Sometimes put me in a relaxing mood.
And the drops that hummed as they fell
Gave off an odor that I loved to smell.

I listened to the patter on the windowpane
And the rhythmic sound of the falling rain.
To the window I was drawn, out of curiosity
And welcomed what I was eager to see.

The drops at times, sprinkled us gently
At other times, they fell heavily.
From a distance, they approached us hastily
As they fell, I imagined they were singing to me.

What Are They

They come with each wave
Reaching for the shore.
Dancing as they draw near
Trying to deliver more.
They number the uncountable.
Together, they hold the fort.
Men cannot outnumber them
Even if they all could float.

These brown, grass-like plants
To our shores, arrive from the sea.
From where in the wide Atlantic
Could these strangers' origins be?
They come without mercy
Making the blue seawater brown
Preventing people from having a bath
They can only look at them and frown.

Here they are on the North American land
Mingling closely with the Florida sand
Having first invaded the Caribbean
Where residents work tirelessly
To remove them completely.
But they keep coming at a steady speed.
These invaders that pay us no heed.
Are known as the Sargassum seaweed!

A Zinnia

I looked through my window and saw
A beautiful flower that put me in awe.
It was a Zinnia, standing tall and proud.
It swayed gently as it looked at white clouds.

This Zinnia wore a crown of pure gold
To which its petals had a hold.
This crown gave it the power
To be the strength of the flower.

The petals sat on the tall green stem
That provided much support for them.
Many young buds were eager to grow
And vie with the beautiful Zinnia's glow.

Mother Nature had adorned them all.
A bee visited her after feeling her call
It sat on her crown, after walking around.
With the golden dust that it recently found.

Then a yellow butterfly caught my eyes
As it ignored the Zinnia and floated by.
My attention returned to the beautiful flower
On whom Nature with beauty had showered.

Tomorrow is another beautiful day.
I wish the Zinnia was here to stay.
It may be weeks before the petals fade
So, in its beauty, I will continue to bathe.

A Flower

Do we appreciate nature?
And do we appreciate a flower
That is a part of Mother Nature?
Some people may see it as a "wild" flower
And to others, it may be "delicately reared."
Whatever we think of that flower
It has been put on earth to give us joy.

Singing Birds

I listen as my pet birds sing.
It seems as if I hear bells ring.
They make music in my ears
And drive away my fears.

Yes, they sing in unison
They make their music into a song.
I pause, and let my ears take in
The melody as my birds sing.

They sing for each other, and for me.
I listen intently, and I see
The beauty in them that God has made
And from my ears their songs won't fade.

Nature

Her thoughts are drawn to nature.
From that you cannot take her.
Her spirit is filled with content.
In nature, her thoughts are spent.

Nature puts her heart at rest.
Strengthens her resolve to resist
The angry thoughts that try to make
Her heart be filled with anger and hate.

Nature gives her relief from stress.
Makes her from evil thoughts digress.
The beautiful things she observes in nature
Allow her to use them as her comforter.

Nature shows the greatness of art.
The sun, moon, and stars for a start.
The majesty of all she sees since her birth
Is her reason for her love of Mother Earth.

My Mind

My mind is adorned with the beauty of nature.
It thinks of the creatures that were made
Many dressed in beautiful colors, with many patterns,
the designs not formed by human imagination.

A Foreigner

She was a foreigner, some said
But here she stayed and was wed.
She had come from a green island
In the Caribbean.
A mountainous green island
From a village with many flowers
Then she, with love, was showered.
She chose to live on this island
That was also a colony of England.
She did not want to live elsewhere.
So in Barbados she came to stay.

My Mother

How can I describe my dear, sweet mother
The woman, who to me, was like no other?
The person, who I early discovered
Was filled with love for me and my brother?

Words cannot express how much I love her.
Why she worked so hard, I often wondered.
Toiling in the hot sun, for us, to secure
A nourishing meal, like the day before.

My mother was alone while striving to feed us.
No family to assist her on the island of Barbados.
She did not complain of the feeling of tiredness
But cared for us with patience and tenderness.

I'm forever filled with admiration for her.
I know that from life, she could have had more.
I think of her hardship and lack of support
And give thanks to God, who allowed her to cope.

Strength

The woman was tall and slender.
She walked upright, with no desire to surrender.
The hardships that attacked her during the years
Did not weaken her faith or drive her to tears.

Strengthened by faith and filled with hope
Toiling daily, trying to cope
Praying for strength as she swiftly walked
And asking for deliverance, with God she talked.

Filled with determination to succeed
She was generous, and often willing to feed
Those who lacked a meal on the day
That she lacked money for her own meals to pay.

A kind, compassionate woman was she
Who prayed daily, and tried to be
Content with what she had and told me
To strive to be good, and the good Lord I'll see.

The Examination

The father of the boy had a goal:
To send his son to a prestigious school.
But to pay his school fee was a challenge.
He did not know how he would manage.

His son was an intelligent child.
Brought up to be studious, he tried
To learn all that his teachers taught
And extra teaching from his father he got.

The time was coming for the test.
The boy studied, and did his best
To retain all that he was taught.
For more knowledge, he seriously sought.

He sat the examination, and he passed.
His father was proud when at last
The school told him his son would get
Free education! He had people's respect!

Eyes

She had special eyes
That were filled with beauty
They glowed with the love
That she showed to her family.

Her eyes were wide and dark.
They fluttered and gave off sparks.
Darting eyes from side to side
Showing their beauty, she could not hide.

They sparkled and did not cast a spell.
Her love for us, they tried to tell.
I will remember those eyes filled with love
Given to her by the One above!

Aunt Marie

There was a lady who was good to me
She told me her name was Aunt Marie.
I was young at the time and did not see
The goodness of Aunt Marie.

She was a gentle lady, was kind to me
The lady whose name was Aunt Marie.
I gradually began to feel and see
The kindness of Aunt Marie

She called my name with a clear, sweet voice.
It beckoned to me, and I had no choice
But to heed the call, and follow the voice
Of the lady who was Aunt Marie.

She accompanied me home, and sat with me
Waited for my parents and my brother to see.
Chatted while my mother prepared a meal
And I happily dined with Aunt Marie.

She left us and travelled across the sea.
The United States with her husband to be
And I hoped that one day I would see
The new country of Aunt Marie.

I think lovingly of that sweet lady
Who showed love and kindness to me
For she did not forget the child who she
Wanted to call her Aunt Marie.

She wrote loving letters to all of us.
I knew that in her I could put my trust.
The gifts that came for my brother and me
Were sent by our angel, Aunt Marie

The kindness she showed to my family
Has planted a lasting deep gratitude in me.
I look at her beautiful photo lovingly
And pray for the soul of Aunt Marie.

Human Beings

This earth is a beautiful planet.
Mankind and animals were put on it.
They have here a special place
Where human beings their bodies disgrace.

Do evil things, make people ashamed.
Find excuses, and others, they blame.
Trying to impress bad influential peers
Taking human lives, and do not care.

Some realize the wrong things they do
Apologize to society, and to you.
Making promises that may come true
Turning from evil, their lives become new.

When you look at their other side
Humans cannot from nature, hide
With the law, they may try to abide
At times, need shelter; on people, rely.

For protection from harm, on God they call.
Since from His arms, they cannot fall.
Yet, disappoint Him, and with others, quarrel
Then, on Him, call, when they're in peril.

With joy, man can discover good things
That positive actions and words can bring
By reaching out to other human beings
Showing love from hearts that praises, sing.

Faces

The women wore their dresses with pride.
Their heads held high; their shoulders wide.
But under their long skirts they tried to hide
The faces of suffering so many despised.

These faces that they carried with pride
Felt much pain and suffering undescribed.
Hidden where no eyes could scan
Those covered up pains made no demands.

The face of hunger was only seen
By the face of sadness under the hem
Of the long, straight skirts that hid them well.
Their suffering and pain, no one could tell.

Forced by hunger and the need for bread
The face of hardship exposed its head.
Its sisters and brothers, hidden from view
Revealed their faces to find food too.

These faces met words of insults and ridicule
But the women worked hard to give them food.
To protect those faces, they felt no shame.
Strong women they were, and with pride reigned.

A Teacher

I used to be a teacher
And I taught the children well.
I did my best to lecture and
Teach them how to spell.

But I lacked more knowledge of the method of control
Of those pupils who kept talking
And not reaching for the goal.

How to add and subtract
Borrow and pay back
Multiply and divide
And from problems not hide.

From self-control they strayed
And sometimes preferred to play
With the objects that they
Used to take away and repay.

They would seek my attention
As they wrestled for an object
That was being used to
Teach them the main subject.

"Please, teacher, I want these!"
"No! I want them!" says another.
"Please, children!" I plead
But of the two, none would heed.

I gained their attention
When I told them, that
If they give and take back
Then they will add and subtract.

My Birthday

Oh, what a joyful day!
I have seen another year
And there is nothing to fear.
My Maker has heard my prayer.

I remain under my doctor's care
And I'm responsible to keep near
Follow his instructions and beware
Of problems that may appear.

So, with you, I share
The happiness I feel today.
And with God, my faith will stay.
He leads me all the way.

Alone

All alone at home.
Sitting by the unopened window
Wishing that someone would visit.
Listening for the sound of footsteps
That climb the creaky wooden steps.
Waiting for a knock at the door
That is left unlocked.

All alone at home.
Hoping for words of
Greetings from relatives, or friends.
Thinking of her mother who
faced the challenges of an illness
And who showered words of love on her.
Oh! How she misses her mother!

The Waif

She walked along the road.
A long, narrow road
A lonely road.
Where are the people?
They are still asleep.
So, why is she not asleep too?
Because she has much to do.
Her errands she must complete.
That is why she is not asleep.
See! She takes her pail
And sets out in her walking shoes
What shoes?
Her barefoot shoes!
And goes up the hill
Yonder!
She had to remember!
To remember what?
To go to houses every morning
And empty the containers
With scraps for the animals.
She had to hurry!
To get on with her walking!
She returned to her place of abode
And continued her routine—
Drink the cold tea.

Yes, tea!
And where is the bread or biscuit?
What bread? What biscuit?
There is none for her!
Then she dresses herself for school.
She must hurry
Or she will be late!

The Child

She found herself in a strange house
Had to keep quiet like a mouse.
To other rooms she dared not walk.
In a low voice she had to talk.

She sat quietly in the dim hallway.
Had no toys with which to play.
No stories to hear; not many words to say.
Was ignored by adults most of the day.

She played alone when in the yard.
Used her imagination, and that was sad.
Used broken cutlery to pay for food
Made with dirt, and that was not good.

Would lay on the floor and try to sleep.
Opened her eyes, and at times peeped
At the one who was paid the child to keep.
Felt hungry and had nothing to eat.

When her mother came for her at night
She felt happy, was out of her plight
Until the next day, when she again
Relived the sadness, felt the pain.

A Simple Girl

A simple girl, they call me!
Why can't they see
The other side of me?
A girl, thoughtful of others
One who thinks about the suffering.
Also knows the lack of bread and butter
As she, too, has known the lack of the latter.

A simple girl, she was called.
Why can't they see the other "she"
Who others' plight could see!
Tries to assist the ailing
Comforts the sad and lonely
But is overlooked by the society
That for her needs has a responsibility.

Rex

Oh! How I grieve for my dog, Rex.
He was adorable, loving, and wonderful.
He was my protector and my companion.
He was my best friend.

I grieve for his unexpected passing
For the joy I have lost at his death.
A death that all must experience
Yet, my dog, Rex, is deeply missed.

For ten years, Rex was my friend.
A true friend that looked.
A faithful friend that listened
To a language that was not his.

Rex made his presence known.
He greeted me upon my arrival home.
From where he stood, I was unseen.
Yet, he knew that I had arrived.

The sound of his bark, light, and calling
Saying: "Hello! I am here!
"How are you? I'm waiting to see you!"
What a friend for one to have!

His illness was short; my grief was long.
He knew that he would be deeply missed.
So he sent another companion to us.
His name is Blackie, and I call him "Rex."

My Dog, Blackie

Have you ever seen a dog laugh?
That is my dog, Blackie!
When I sing, he smiles.
How do I know he smiles?
He shows it in his eyes.
His teeth are all exposed.
And he grins with a shiny nose.
He lies on his side
With his four legs in repose
Stretched out before him.
His head rests on the ground
With his eyes staring into space
Yet Blackie is listening intently to my song.

Blackie

Blackie, why call him "Blackie"?
Because he was black!
A black dog with a mauve tongue
And personality he did not lack.

Blackie was a serious dog.
He was alert and he was shy.
He was swift, but he was cautious
Was possessive, and I wondered why.

Blackie was a stray dog.
He was a lonely dog.
He was a hungry, tired dog.
But he became a happy, content dog.

Blackie was a faithful dog.
He was my best friend.
He was my husband's best friend.
Blackie was a companion for the lonely.

Blackie could make one laugh.
He liked to fetch and bring the ball.
But there were some other things
He did not like to do at all.

Blackie had a personality.
He listened to my singing attentively.
When invited. to show his moves
Blackie danced for me.

Blackie was a true friend of man.
He was a patient, loving dog.
When we walked, and with a friend I talked
My attention he sought by licking my hand.

Me

I see myself from child to adult
And I've wondered why
So many times
I was showered with insults.
But time has passed
And here I am, a woman
Who has overcome!
And through my challenges I've lasted.
I've overcome the shyness.
How it occurred, only God knows.
I hope my grace to show
As I walk along the narrow path.
I thank God for His guidance
For allowing me to think clearly
To speak wisely
To have good thoughts
And be helpful to my neighbors.

Give Thanks

It may sound quite simple
Or may only be a word.
But it needs to be heard:
"Thanks!"

It may not mean much
But the word says a lot.
Because we must for all things
Give thanks!

We do not mean to over speak.
Although when we are about to eat
We bow our heads with gratitude and
Give God thanks!

In everything we do or say
We thank the Lord that we may
Have the grace to pray, and tell Him
"Thanks!"

The Rock

I've come home to you my dearest friend.
The longing to see you has come to an end.
You, my island home, known as "The Rock"
Is situated in what I call a "special spot."

The wide ocean stretches far to the east.
I stare in the distance, and my mind can't cease
To marvel at how this piece of beloved rock
Has become so loved that many to it flock.

You are sitting calmly in the Atlantic Ocean,
Looking across the blue Caribbean sea.
And there…you have sisters, neighbors too,
That are part of the union that includes you.

You are alone in this calm atmosphere.
Peaceful and soothing many are aware.
They come, like I do, to sit in the sun
To dance to Soca and Calypso and have fun.

My Island Home

See how the Lord has blessed us!
We are in our homeland, Barbados!
An island adorned with a special beauty
Situated just outside the Caribbean Sea.

This land that means so much to me
Always on my mind, Bim, I wanted to see
To visit places of interest, admire the city
See the annoying animal, the Green Monkey!

I love to see the yellow and green grass
In some areas where I drive past.
They sway in the gentle, refreshing breeze
And send a soothing message to me.

The ocean that is very deep and wide.
Rushes in to greet us on the Atlantic side
With waves that give alto and base-like roars
As they dash against the sandy shores.

They stretch their arms and cover the sand.
I watch with pleasure as children run
From frothy waves that lash at their feet.
This memory of Barbados I want to keep.

This island, surrounded by the blue Atlantic
Has a special beauty, and I've come to watch it.
The areas where the picturesque cliffs stand
Staring at the dark-blue water in the distance.

Many people eagerly come and watch
The rolling waves from their special spot
They stand like statues while taking in
The approaching waves that are glistening.

I will always love this isle of mine.
Knowing I can return to it and find
The comfort I need when nostalgia comes
Far from Barbados, my island home.

Barbados, Its Strengths

There is more than one way
Where homage to our nation we can pay.
Our country deserves to be treated
Like the isle where visitors are cordially greeted.

Tourism industry we must put first
To fill our beautiful homeland's purse.
So we must continue, and in many ways
Try to make this industry all our bills pay.

Education for all is surely a must!
It is what will continue to give a plus
To the financial growth of the nation
Due to the "good brains" of the citizens.

Democracy and equal opportunity let people see
How important prosperity and growth must be.
While promoting our island, we must agree
That we, not disadvantaged people, are free.

Values and morals may appear last
But must never be a heavy task.
Without good morals we lose our grasp
And find many people having to fast.

In my homeland, what is found
Is the best that is not tossed around.
Special qualities that are so sweet
That we, in Barbados, we must keep.

We can go on and on until we reach
The top of the pinnacle that is steep.
Our high qualities we must retain
So that our nation can avoid grief and pain.

When challenges come, we must remember
To value our statesmen, and to them render
Praises and thanks, while to others unknown
Show gratitude for preserving our isle, our home.

My homeland, an isle, is described as small.
When, in fact, it has goals that are very tall.
Tall and filled with all that would
Sustain the nation with all that is good.

It has so much, that it is high
Its climbing goals seem to reach for the sky.
And inside the belly of this nation
Are stored all the good qualities for our children.

Foolish Love

You may say I'm a fool
To let men treat me like they do.
I will tell these words to you.
The one I love has me confused.
I allow him my heart to abuse.

Love catches at my throbbing heart.
It makes Cupid's arrow into it dart.
The love I feel is very strong.
I do not care if it's right or wrong.
For me, this love will last long.

My foolish heart is made to love
Love makes me coo, just like a dove.
Love makes my heart merrily sing.
In my lovesick head, the church bells ring.
To him, my heart will always cling.

I will let my love live on!
It is what keeps me feeling young.
In the falling rain and the rising sun
I feel like life has just begun.
In his arms I will forever run.

Dreams

Some dreams disturb me in my sleep.
They make me wake and start to weep.
Some of the memories I cannot keep.
The feelings they bring are very deep.

I ponder on what I had dreamed
And the interpretations, at times, seemed
As if the dream would mean
That what I dreamed would soon be seen.

Although some dreams make me sad
Others, at times, make me glad.
And although some dreams were bad
I reflected on all the dreams I had.

I feel happy when I awake
And to my family can relate.
The dream that to me seemed to say
My mind will be at peace on that day

Telling

I could tell you many things
That to my soul joy brings.
There are so many that I find
I need to sort them in my mind.

There is so much in this world
That can bring joy to our soul.
We only need to find the time
And try to sort them in our mind.

Many things that we remember
From January up to December
Can put a big smile on our face
And in our soul give us grace.

Some of the memories make us sad
And, deprive us of the joy we had.
But if on our Maker we earnestly call
He will not allow us, into despair, fall.

If we look back, we can surely see
That God has been good to you and me.
As we sort them out, the good and bad
We can thank Him for what we have.

See and Think

When we are alone, our thoughts tend to wander.
We think of everything except our Heavenly Father.
It is when the conditions in our lives give us grief
That we turn to Him and plead for some relief.

His loving mercy guides us, and to us He shows
The way in life we should let our thoughts flow.
We follow the path our mind tells us to take
And try to avoid our previous mistakes to make.

But temptation raises its head and looks at us.
Tries its best evil thoughts and acts on us to thrust
That we will see what appears to be beckoning
Drawing us to the pit, where we can fall into sin.

We must think wisely and don't allow the enemy
To take control of our passions and not let us see
The errors in our thoughts, actions, and inactions.
Praying ceaselessly, let us ask our God for protection.

Thinking Too Much

Why do you think so much, my friend?
If you have problems, pray they end.
Thinking is good most of the time
But too much of it can ruin your mind.

Try not to think of problems, just pray!
It can give relief from a very stressful day
Because only your Creator can take it away.
Without His presence, you have no say.

Your mind needs to rest so that it can cope
With the stress that your thoughts overtake.
For you to overcome so much thinking
Have faith in God, and on Him, keep calling.

Our Garden

In our garden, the plants had many flowers
That were adorned with different colors.
In the soil, where our energy was often spent
We were enveloped with a feeling of content
That the flowering plants gave joy to others.

Some people stopped to admire the flowers.
At times they chose to cut what was ours.
We, at times, offered young plants to them
Gave advice on managing their garden
Interest, they lacked; could not be bothered!

In our garden, we often took long walks.
About the flowering plants, we had long talks.
About their beauty that gave such joy.
We feasted on their beauty with eager eyes
Discovering what nature to us had brought.

Pray for Grace

Do not let the words of man influence you.
You must imagine their intentions too.
Think twice before anything you do.
About what will not be beneficial to you.

Sometimes we follow the actions of others
Looking for quick solutions to our sorrows.
But the strong temptation to do what is bad
Becomes the problem that makes us sad.

Praying for strength and calling to God
Is what we need to protect us, lest we fall.
When we go through rough times
We must have the grace of God on our mind.

Giving Thanks

I thank my Maker for all I have.
For keeping me from what is bad.
No need to complain; He has made me whole
He's the Comforter for my sin-sick soul.

He has kept me alive to see this age.
Allowed me to fail and turn a new page
That tells me to call out to Him when in need.
He will hear my cry; my needs He will heed.

There may be days when life is rough.
To find food for all may sometimes be tough.
But in God, we must always place our trust.
He will send His angels to take care of us.

The Mind

Can anyone find
The actions of the mind?
Who can be so inclined
To explain the actions of the mind!

The mind is an invisible being
That one has no hope of seeing.
It is a strange creature
And it has the qualities of a thinker.
By man it cannot be controlled.
We cannot monitor or assess it
Neither can we put a hand on it.
Of it, we can lose control
But on us it can have a hold.
When we humans make a fuss
It is our mind directing us.

It is a powerful spirit
Doctors try to control it.
Grace and the Holy Ghost
Is the controller of our mind.
Peace, through God, it will find.

Wishing

As I sail on the wide blue sea
I become as relieved as I possibly can be
Taking in the fresh air
Not having a care
Happy as I can be
And wishing that you could be here with me!

I listen to the music, watch people dance.
Watch the limbo movements
How people prance
To the rhythmic sound
Of the deep throbbing drums
And I wish you could be here with me!

The singers in the band are very good.
Their different voices
Make me think that I could
Sing alto like some of them do.
My voice was not good, this I could not see.
And l wish you could have been here with me.

I hope to be home soon, and you, I'll see.
You do not know
How happy I will be!
Being alone on a ship at sea
Is a lonely and sad experience for me.
I long with you to be
And feel your presence here with me.

Awareness

I stood still in my garden and paid attention.
I watched as the leaves on the trees glistened.
To the birds as they sang, I happily listened.
For these blessings I looked up to heaven.

The singing birds were joined by others.
Together they sang, appearing like a choir.
As their music in my ears continued to ring
I suddenly realized it was the beginning of spring!

Watching

She watches him as he sleeps.
She gazes and gazes
Not moving
From where she stands
Thinking deeply as she gazes.

He is sleeping soundly.
His chest rises and falls
As he breathes in and out.

All is well in that quiet room.
No sound of snoring.
Only gentle breathing!
He is not aware that
He is being gazed upon with love.

Thanks to Nature

Allow your mind to be opened
To the possibilities of thought
That to you may be brought.
The feelings, the emotions
That can lead to different actions.
The beauty that we discover
In the wonders of nature.
Plants, animals, and other creatures
In our thoughts, allow us to act
Compassionate, and it's a fact!
Let us give praises and thanks
For the joys that we feel
And the hurts that can be healed.
Give thanks for what we observe.
Give thanks for our five senses
That let us discover the beauty of nature.

Hungry and Content

He was sitting all alone
In a corner
And he was talking with
An unseen person.
His conversation was loud.
He gave instructions
And acted as though
He was receiving orders too.
But to whom was he talking?
It was an imaginary friend.
He was happy with his friend.
But did he have a meal this morning?
No. He did not eat.
Yet he played with his friend
His invisible friend!
He appeared content.
But the man had to give him a meal!
From where could he find it?
There was nothing in the house!
He walked the street and found a shop
He bought nourishment for the boy.
And he was fed on that day.
But what about the days to come?

God Is with You

When God is with you, have no fear.
You may not have family or friends near.
Remember! Although you cannot see Him
If you listen, you can hear His voice within

God is with to you, even though you may
Not realize how much for you He cares.
He watches as you kneel and to Him pray
And listens to all you have to say.

He knows your words before you speak.
He looks out for you, when food you seek.
You may not realize, but when you are weak
God gives you strength to stand on your feet.

So put your Creator first in everything you do.
When you are in danger, He will protect you.
He is with you when challenges enter your life.
And directs your path when you encounter strife

Gratitude

Is it wrong to be grateful?
And to show that you are not hateful?
Is it wrong to express how you feel?
To tell who caused your body to heal?

Was it you who felt the gratitude
And could not control your attitude
As you wrote the words you chose
To give thanks, to compose.

Yes, I wrote those expressive lines.
They tell of the reflective times
When I felt such great relief
My family did not have to grieve.

Conflict

Throughout our lives we can find
Some people tend to be unkind.
Sometimes an effort is made to find
What goes on in their hateful mind.

Some people just want to be evil
They do not make any effort to be civil.
They let temptation from the devil
Make them with others fight and quarrel.

When we try to show them our best
They ignore us and become unjust.
Swords filled with insults at us they thrust.
Run from their weapons of pain, we must!

Their biting words are filled with spite
And in their hearts, they feel delight.
But we, the victims, pray that they might
Change their evil ways by asking God for insight.

Strive

Try to overcome your fears
Wipe away your tears
Open your ears, and
Listen!

Listen to your thoughts.
Know that you ought
To retain what was taught, and
Believe!

Believe that you are loved
By your Father, the One above.
For He alone can solve your
Problems!

He gave you a mind
So that you can find
The way to a kind of
Solution!

So put God first.
Don't allow the curse
Of evil to burst your
Bubble!

Cast evil aside
And for goodness' sake
Strive to do your best as you live
Daily!

My Explanation

These thoughts that often come to me
Flow freely because of the reality
That the Heavenly Father allows me to be
Alive! He has set my thoughts free.

Peace to me comes because of this.
I cannot say how much I will miss
Expressing my emotions to all of you
This path I take, God will see me through.

The challenges that come my way each day
Are part of my life, this I can truly say.
I give the Almighty thanks, and I pray
My faith will remove my challenges today.

About the Author

Letitia was born on the island of Barbados, West Indies. She has a special love for her homeland, from where her roots of coping with challenges in life have stayed throughout the years. Her education was obtained at St Patrick's RC school and the Modern High School in Bridgetown, Barbados.

This is her first attempt at publishing her thoughts.

Her religious upbringing and the determination of her parents to give her and her brother a secondary education, have led to her present status as the writer of *Letitia's Thoughts in Verse*. She was a teacher of infants and juniors before immigrating to England to become a registered nurse, where she advanced her studies in midwifery, intensive care, and psychiatry. She has worked in French-speaking Canada, before settling in the USA. She received her bachelor of health service administration at Florida International University.

Letitia has been described as a "still water that runs deep." She loves poetry and describes nature in poetic words. Being a shy teenager, she engrossed herself in interesting books, some being the biographies of influential people. She also enjoyed writing essays. She has written short skits for educational purposes and has shared some of her verses with friends who have encouraged her to publish them. Her greatest hobby is gardening.

Letitia is retired. She and her husband, Clifford, spend their leisure time traveling and gardening.

CPSIA information can be obtained
at www.ICGtesting.com
Printed in the USA
LVHW111746120720
660466LV00004B/636